Previous Books By Patrick Sylvain

Unfinished Dreams / Rèv San Bout (bilingual poetry)
Education Across Borders
Underworlds
Love, Lust, & Loss / Lanmou, anvi, pèdans (bilingual poetry)

Books Written in Haitian "Creole":

Masuife
Anba Bòt Kwokodil
Zansèt
Maryaj Ide ak Imajinasyon

FIRE

ON

THE

TONGUE

poems

ARROWSMITH

Fire on the Tongue
Patrick Sylvain

© 2026 Patrick Sylvain
All Rights Reserved

ISBN: 979-8-9915254-3-5

Library of Congress Control Number: 2026901177

Boston — New York — San Francisco — Baghdad
San Juan — Kyiv — Istanbul — Santiago, Chile
Beijing — Paris — London — Cairo — Madrid
Milan — Melbourne — Jerusalem — Darfur

11 Chestnut St.
Medford, MA 02155

arrowsmithpress@gmail.com
www.arrowsmithpress.com

The seventy-fourth Arrowsmith book was typeset & designed by
Gerard Robertson for Askold Melnyczuk & Alex Johnson in Garamond
Font

FIRE

ON

THE

TONGUE

poems

PATRICK SYLVAIN

CONTENTS

Part One

1- Constellation	17
2- The Island Self	18
3- No Requiems	19
4- Pyramid of Words	20
5- Crossroads	21
6- Star Apple	22
7- Custard Apple	24
8- Boiling Space	26
9- Choreography Of Discipline	28
10- Stanzas & Sawdust	31
11- Allure of the Caribbean	33
12- The Roasted Goat	36
13- Miles of Remembrance, 1978	40
14- Neighbor's Garden	42
15- North Atlantic Circus	43

Part Two

16- Navigating	49
17- Windows of Exile	52
18- Marooning	54
19- Elegy for My Father	56
20- Unexpected	58
21- Echoes of Home, 1991	60
22- Rebirth	62
23- New York, NY	65
24- Denial	66
25- Existing	67
26- Semblance	69
27- Searing Daggers	71
28- Epidermopolis	73
29- A Night in Brooklyn	75
30- History of Laments	77
31- Canonized Token	79
32- Blue Blood	80

Part Three

33- The Coffin Maker & The Poet	85
34- Contumelious	89
35- Benedictus	91
36- Logos	92
37- Congestion	93
38- Convulsion	94
39- Centuries of Ashes	95
40- Cocoon of Poverty	96
41- Boulevard Jean-Jacques Dessalines	98
42- A Palace of Mourners	99
43- Grieving	101
44- Prolongation	102
45- Cracked	103
46- Haiti: A Disavowal	105
47- Confluence	107
48- Menelik	108
49- Secret of La Sirène	109

50- Jujubean	111
51- Polarization	113
52- Theseus' Shield	114
53- Underworld Enterprise	116
54- Thirty-one Years	119
55- Invocation	122
56- The Magic of Rhythm	124
57- Cantor of The Irish Spring	125
58- Boston Capitol Steps, 1987	127
59- Over the Salt & Pepper Bridge	128
60- Supreme	129
61- Illumination, A Sonnet	130
62- Terra Blanca	131
63- Scorching Dreams	132
64- Home, a Desire	133

ACKNOWLEDGEMENTS

The following poems, or versions of them, have appeared in: *Caribbean Writer* ("Crossroads"); *Calabash: A Journal of Caribbean Arts & Letters* ("Marooning"); *Crab Orchard Review* ("Windows of Exile", "Pyramid of Words"); *Haitian Times* ("The Coffin Maker & The Poet"); *Jet Fuel Review* ("Stanzas and Sawdust"); *Step Into A World: A Global Anthology Of New Black Literature* ("Windows of Exile"); *PBS NewsHour* ("Century of Ashes, Boulevard Jean-Jacques Dessalines, Cocoon of Poverty"); *Poets for Haiti: An Anthology of Poetry and Art* ("Boulevard Jean-Jacques Dessalines"); *SpoKe 11* ("Invocation," "The Magic of Rhythm," "Cantor of The Irish Spring," "Boston Capitol Steps, 1987," "Existing," "A Night of Injustice"); *SX Salon* ("No Requiems"); *The Heartland Review* ("Jujubean"); *The Poets are Gathering - Benjamin Boone* (A Poetry and Jazz CD "Marooning," "The Magic of Rhythm"); *TINT Journal* ("The Magic of Rhythm"); *Transition* ("The Coffin Maker & The Poet"); *Verity La* ("Rebirth").

I would like to extend a special thanks to my wife and close friend, Jalene, for her support and always my first reader. I would also like to thank the members of Langston's Legacy Poetry Collaborative for their friendships and keen eyes: Danielle Legros-Georges, Florence Ladd, Gavin Moses, Joshua Bennett, Andrea Bossi, LaTasha Diggs, Nicole Terez Dutton.

I'm also very thankful for having studied under Robert Pinsky at Boston University, and also thankful to Henri Cole and Dan Chiasson for their comments and suggestions.
Thanks to: Sandy Alexandre, Tina Beyene, Jenny Factor, Djeunie Saint-Louis, Gina Désir, Edwidge Danticat, Yusef Komunyakaa, Martín Espada, Eileen Pun, Tomas Unger, Sutopa Dasgupta, Fred Marchant, Lloyd Schwartz, Askold Melnyczuk, members of the Dark Room Collective, Tony Bogues, Dante Micheaux, and my traveling guides. Finally, thanks to the dynamic team at Arrowsmith Press.

"In accumulating property for ourselves or our posterity, in founding a family or a state, or acquiring fame even, we are mortal; but in dealing with truth we are immortal, and need fear no change nor accident."

— Henry David Thoreau
Walden. Ch.3, Reading

Part One

"*Obruni* forced me to acknowledge that I didn't belong anyplace. The domain of the stranger is always an elusive *elsewhere.*"
—Saidiya Hartman
Lose Your Mother

Constellation

I grew up in the sweltering heat among a proliferation
of sugar cane, among imported mannerisms that buckled
the freedom of youth. I was raised within a constellation
of wails, shouts, laughter, and silences. I flourished among
a galaxy of minds, genuises, genies and unlettered eyes
bursting with knowing like clear channels of radio waves.
I listened. I grew up with a universe of stars manifesting
a code of politeness through arranged doilies beneath delicate
gold-rimmed china plates and polished silverware, forging
attitudes. My latitude became more distant from the center
as I placed the host on my agnostic tongue. At the table, crucified
by my aunt's cutting stares, I felt like a heathen when my gaze
hinted at questioning heaven. The dining room amplifying
her mid-range dramatic contralto: "Young man, watch
your tongue. This is a Christian household." Canoodling
my thoughts, I was immersed in the depths of wonder
before the logarithmic spirals of nautili, forming
a labyrinth of ephemeral splendor where life and
death meet in an embrace. Despite the scalding of whips
and scoldings, I grew up questioning tongues praising
genuises along a congregation of crucifixes and saints.

The Island Self

My eyes capture but cannot shutter the light
Of childhood flooding the shores of self.

My muse, a broken homeland lodged deep,
Flickers in the mind and the spine.

To silence it is to cease existing,
A song burrowed in the ear's inner chamber.

No phonograph needed; such love never dies,
It is the cureless hurt, a dictatorial spring

declaring itself eternal. I cannot walk away
From the shore of myself; I'm already an island,

Rooted deeply in the archipelago of memories, where
Each egret leaping is an age of tenderness and knowing.

No Requiems

The childrens' voices dive
with the crashing waves
and hollering west wind.
The old folks with kachimbo
pipes puff tobacco
as their toothless mandibles
masticate on the memories
of promising words.
Freedom.
The promise of heaven
is its own trapdoor.
Silence—the cemeteries here
are hungry pelicans
with no symphony
to sing requiems
for dead fishes.
Dead fishes, we are.
The gluttonous sea
vomited us here
on these wailing islands,
and the seagulls fear our shrills.

Pyramid Of Words

I seek words when words speak memory,
memories of Columbus unleashing his swords,
planting seeds of violence in the midst of tribes.

I seek words to speak for scorched tongues,
In a country where pain burns from bones that beat,
for life, where nightsticks crack skulls, spreading terror.

I seek words to cleanse the infection of the conquerors'
languages, their long vowels of repression: the A's,
the I's and the O's screaming in the night.

I seek spicy words to feed stale tongues of zombies,
so the eyes of peasants on donkeys' backs can read
themselves out of ignorance, entering pyramids
of words, unlocking the secrets of syntax.

Crossroads

Grandpa's thick brown leather belt struck
when I forgot verses in Latin and threw
the hardcover book into the wooden latrine.

At school, when French lessons were difficult to recite,
a dry, thin cowhide, coiled into an Igwaz,
pinched my thighs, leaving worm-sized bruises.

I feared books. Words were like pebbles in my eyes;
as their syllables rang, my vision blurred on every page.
Uninterested, my mind wandered to the soccer ball

bouncing in the street. I wanted to kick
the book, but I was under grandpa's tall frame
and fiery stare. I read—dragging my mind along the pages.

I did not know words could stretch like shadows,
like the long hand of a slow clock elongating my punishment,
needles of syllables tightening around my neck.

Now, at the throat of a crossroad,
I write, reaching for a familiar language
to voice the pain of mouths silenced by nightsticks.

At the crossroads of poetry and prose,
where lyrics are hands clapping life into the forgotten,
I write to dance beyond frontiers of pineapples and bananas.

Where the arms of world literature extend
to catch the ringing of syllables, like leaves
telling how fierce the Western wind blows.

Star Apple
In memoriam F.P.

Purplish red, plump, organically grown
the star apple was a star among
the fruit bearing tropical trees. Bird

and human eyes minding for ripeness.
The star apple tree radiated
splendor, verdant and lush

with simple, oval, evergreen leaves.
Tiny purplish-white flowers adorned
its outer shell, emitting desirous fragrance.

I was bewitched, seduced by the hermaphroditic
star, its dark purple fruit, breast-milk sweet,
sticky star-patterned pulp with hard,

oily, brown, flattened seeds that rolled
around my tongue like ambrosia.
Hard slaps behind the back of the head

brought me back to Grandpa's landscape.
A hummingbird whirred in my head
until I saw the unhappiness of his star.

The garden was my paradise:
coconut, mandarin, cherry, pomegranate,
custard apple, and the delicious star apple.

I watched Grandpa knife through
the dense purple skin to reach soft pulp,
then neatly arrange the seedless slices

on yellow Tupperware for his mulatto
Madame who insatiably consumed everything
we loved, even our milky, scrumptious star apples.

Custard Apple (Kachiman)
In memoriam F.P.

You hung there for two weeks, fourteen feet above
the ground, four feet from the neighbor's
kitchen roof, and six feet from the fence wall.
Rocks, dead wood made the climb easy.

The pinkish-red glow and cow's heart shape
formed the perfect pendant. The garden
was a verdant waiting room. No wind,
I waited for you to drop. Then, a craving
came from my gut. I ventured to the roof
to look closely at the long oval patterns
clustered all over your pine cone-like shape.

Sweet, soft, slightly granular, and gooey.
I closed my eyes. Nose close to the skin,
I inhaled your sweet and ripe fragrance. I touched
your thin tip, yellowish-red, and envisioned
your compacted seeds enveloped in white flesh.

Besides the birds and crickets, I was alone.
I'm not sure who whispered in Grandpa's ears,
or perhaps he had been eyeing the same custard.

But went to the yard determined,
poking hook stick at hand, his eyes turning red

when he saw the stumped stem, empty. He knew
whom to blame. Half eaten, grapefruit size
was still on the table. With cowhide whips,
he made my legs and butt sing for mercy.

Then, calmly like an expert derider, he ordered me
to climb back and hang the other half of the Kachiman.
An audience gathered to eye my anguished steps.
I lassoed the stem as it hung waiting for fruit bats.

Boiling Space

The man who could have taught me love
had an extended whip of an arm, whipping
stalks of legs into shaved canes, bleeding.

I embraced my future with tears and gritted
teeth as nights brought interrogations into
a churning space, a river advancing within me.

The man who could have taught me love
had his own bit to bite when chaos swarmed
his home after an army of hornets took over

the family's vast land in Paillant, hauling
rich earth encrusted with bauxite. A site
of destruction ensued as lives were gun-whipped

to submission. Bitterness grew from his spine
and infected his love ventricles. Rejected by his
in-laws for his tanned mango-skin and calloused

hands, he hammered anguish like nails into
his home, sandpapering order to a smooth finish.
A barrack of a man, he was. Emotions well quartered.

By the time I was born, laughter had burrowed into
a face turned marble by imprisonment and confiscation
of the source of his pride: a 200-man furniture shop.

His own rapids ran through him as he scolded
loved ones with mere contacts. As a buoyant boy,
ignorant of his past, I turned the house into my resort

shuttling the hallways as if I were a conveyer of delight.
My happiness soon quivered at Grandpa's mercy while
raising me with an ominous masked-face. My innocence

sailed through the heart of fear as coarse leather belts
welted thighs into a dance of fire. A boiling space
ran through me as he turned my life into a ballad

of sorrow. And through his own constellation
of pain, he wanted my memories to remain
on a permanent shore, wafted by his presence.

Choreography of Discipline
For Grandpa F. P.

Tall and thin like a plank, yellow,
you were at the center of my grief.

My fingers had just begun holding quills,
so poetic ink could not ooze globules

of pain. Terror emitted from your eyes
as you hovered over me like an omen.

You wanted a man erected from a boy,
my legs sculpted by staccatoed lashes.

You were a maestro of construction,
wood and metal mesh wielded to your measures.

I took note of how you slowly bent cedar
and smoothed out protrusions so precious wood

wouldn't be wasted. It was my job to collect
and separate the scraps by type and shape.

Wicker baskets filed along the back wall
of the depot room, where you once placed

a coffin for a relative who died in New York
but desired tropical ground for burial.

Within a week, you sawed through an entire acajou,
the precise cuts and delicate curves cleaved

rendered you a virtuoso at shaping refractory
elements into functional objects. Refractory,

I was. At twelve, playing marbles or football
was more important than sandpapering handles.

I remember the afternoon when you bruised
my right thigh for leaving the polish undone.

A twisted cowhide, colonial whip became
your fearful baton while imploring

light mahogany-colored legs to instruct
your will. I hated the mean grips that twisted

my ears, inclined to your choreography of discipline.
You yearned for a calibrated mortise and tenon,

a perfectly fitted mold and peg to adjoin your
faultless regiment. With just a hacksaw, a clean-

bladed plane, and your soft filers, you instructed
my own joint making: lap, mortise and tenon.

But I couldn't be shaped into submission
the way wood, cane fiber, and metal mesh did.

I was strong-willed like a bent mason nail,
those whose shanks you hated to redress.

The more you pounded, the more I resisted.
What was the point of making me stand

in front of that empty mahogany coffin?
I shuddered not out of fear, but because of

the gripping hunger and stabbing sun that broke
my will. I knew you were not one to dilute

your inflictive pain. Your cans of primers and paint
were never diluted. You favored purity because

your reputation had to remain stellar. Long hours
spent meshing cane for your prized rattan chairs.

Your choreography of discipline was unbearable,
and after a crescendo of wood-stripping

cracks, I had to adjust under the clamping weight
of callused fingers. Your gripping hands mastered

stubbornness. I slowly became transfixed by your
reverence for structure. My hands mirrored yours.

When I build my own bookshelves, or steady a line,
I'm reminded they should always be flush fitting.

Stanzas & Sawdust
For Grandpa F. P.

Our birthdays were two days apart; we were distant
Gemini. I was always cheery, and you were gloomy, like
an overcoat of mastic. Uncle Ed told me you used
to joke; you were your employees' sap and heartwood.

I wish I had known the non-acrid you, the unfurrowed
brow of your impossible face that I grew reluctant to read.
I wish I had played with those aging knuckles and callused
hands that shaped happiness and pain. Presidents sat on

your chairs, signed contracts on your desks, and hung their
vests inside your flawless mahogany armoires. You were
history. In the 1950s, you were among the top five carpenters
in the country and commanded two hundred employees, until

a whirlwind swept in as dictator, a man you once denied
a seat. Memories of the past went foxhunting.
You were high-yellow and successful, his brand of Noirisme
was sawdust in the people's eyes. It was 1957.

By the time I met you, the workmen were long gone,
and you had been hauled off to the penitentiary. A short stay,
powerful clients pried open the system and implored you to
make a chair—a signatory cane cabriolet armchair for the Doc.

We laughed at how tough you were with your six-foot thin frame.
I remember you smelling of wood—at times pine, cedar, mahogany.
At other times, it was the scent of glue, red chestnut.
With you, the barnyard of my childhood vanished as idleness was

mutinous. A man's life ought to be upright and dignified. Poets
and politicians were blurry. My father was a poet who loved
politics and couldn't use tools the way you did. You were cynical
and the dictator's spectacle chiseled your bliss to the bones.

If you had known of my compact to poetry, that I never inherited
the clamoring gift of turning poles into smooth tapering shafts,
my creativity would have been suffocated in a whirlwind of sawdust.
To you, hands were not made to construct stanzas.

Warm touches only for finished banisters & fluted dowels.
I used to watch your hands run blades over planks, curled
shavings flipping under the motion of your brawny arms.
They formed an ocean of golden waves engulfing your feet.

Now, I know why you used to quip, shut off the radio before
Duvalier blared. You preferred the cascading of sweat on your brow
as you measured your joints to fit frames. Some of your poet friends
vanished while trying to unveil the sun in metered forms.

Allure of the Caribbean

As a child, despite my grandpa's disciplinary
belt, I felt the ocean's allure,
the thrill of the waves rocking my body,
or thundering slaps against rocks,
then the waning echo of suction as if
swallowing its last gulp.
Minutes later, new waves repeated
nature's symphony. I would hoot.

Over the years, the Caribbean Sea became
my secret companion.
Beyond the rolling waves, the salty mists
against my face, I grew to love what I feared.
Underneath the blue wonder of life,
lurked death. Eat and be eaten, the paradox
of existence, the way passion and fury cohabitate.

I lived about a mile from two palm-crowned beaches:
"Ideal Domain", and "White Woman" (Fanm Blanch)
where Canadian tourists once flocked and flopped
their bodies to be baked by the sun.
There, some swam with us naked,
encouraging our native eyes to take in their foreign
glow, their nightly flow with local flesh.

I was too young to go into the clubs,
but despite my grandfather's belt, I learned
to swim against the tide, to climb the rocks
and fearlessly dive into the warm depths
like a scud without tainting my form.
Then, one late afternoon, I was challenged
by a girl, two years older, Canadian, topless and cocky.

Her athletic body with broad shoulders signaled
a stoutness that I discovered only after we dove.
Eighteen feet on the highest rock, we were
expected to swim strokeless under water for fifty feet.

Perfect dive and perfect entry, but after thirty feet
my swimming skill reached its peak. I panicked
when a young man's limp body flashed
and broke open my memory screen.
Two months prior, his body was pulled
from the slow-rocking sea, lifeless as ringing
screams stunned the air. We were not friends,
but I recognized his bow-legged walk.
The gaped mouth and half-open eyes that had been
imprinted in the crevices of my brain flicked
to the surface when I needed air the most.

Taut muscles, ribcage compressed, stinging eyes,
I felt the gravity of the water like shore-waves,
heaved back to the sea. I took a deep breath
and drifted downward. My acumen surrendered,
and I descended, wanting to hit bottom,
until a pair of hands were against my soles, thrusting
me upward like a hurdling fish. I gasped.

When my vision cleared, Pauline was facing me
with a concerned look, our bodies touched.
I thanked her, and we slowly swam sidestroke towards
the cove. Dusk streaked the sky when my feet should
have been jetting home. But Pauline kept me planted.
The warmness of our bodies, pockets of air and salt
of the sea made us one. Until Zeus's thunderbolt
exploded from my spine and made me quiver for mercy.

By the time I reached home, it was past sunset, and Grandpa's belt was the welcoming sentinel. I closed my eyes, clenched my teeth, and took in a storm of lashes. His denouncing voice drowned out as my brain was lulled by waves. That night, I dreamt of an elated mermaid luring me back to the cove where my new Canadian maiden awaited another dive.

The Roasted Goat

Six a.m. on the Southern National Route,
My father, brothers, and I were lulled by the sounds
Of watery fingers playing hide-and-seek,
Lapping slow-to-rouse groves and thickets.
I sat on the back seat of my father's Land Cruiser,
Wedged between an emerald sea of sugarcane and
The Caribbean. Aroma of crushed pulp filtered the air,
Not yet bearing midday's heavy languishing.

As dad shifted gears, my eyes absorbed the vista:
A brown-shirted man pushing a wheelbarrow
With containers of rum, a woman dressed in white
Sipping coffee from a white enamel cup, a bare-chested
Man striking a bullwhip against his herd of cows.
The blues of the ocean beckoning our embrace,
But we had three more plantations, one public market,
And a turbulent river to cross.

A cattle-drawn wagon filled with sugarcane appeared
On the main road; dad pointed to the mills, the remnants
Of a French colony where lives were cut short, crushed
By six days of the whip and bone-hammering labor.
The details of brutality vanished by crushing years, but
Blades of sugarcane leaves still cut workers' skins
As they toiled for a mere breath of existence.
Old plantations morphed into the vagueness of a city,
Where streets were once paths carved for carts and carriages.

Dad shifted gears; we passed a modern motel
With pinkish-red fresco walls, and then a small blue
Painted schoolhouse. Just at the outskirts of the town,
A little boy ventured onto the road with a wheel

Tube and a guiding stick. "Tonnerre de Dieu!"
God's thunder! Father yelled as we veered to the right
Toward an almond tree, and then quickly swerved to the left,
A loud whack silenced our voices before screams
Brought the morning to a commotion. The engine idled.

I climbed out on my father's side with quaking feet,
Where a pool of blood was visible beside a man's
Shoulder. There was litter on the road, a pair of dirty
Sandals, as fear curdled in Frantz' eyes, signaling
For Gerald and me to get back into the car.
My dread crucified to an imagined death. Machetes
Were raised like winged serpents. A man with missing
Front teeth glowered, shouting unholy words at dad.

By the time the shouts subsided and the crowd
Dispersed, I saw dad counting dollar bills.
Twelve, maybe fifteen, certainly more than the man
Would earn in a month. Large banana leaves
Were brought with pieces of rope, then I saw
The bloody black head of a male goat, mangled,
Its matted bulging eyes gawking like a drunk.
Someone wiped the red blotches off the fender,
Handshakes exchanged. A lifeless goat hoisted,
Tied and wrapped in green leaves on the white roof.

Back on the road, we joked about the dead goat
And predicted the many stories it would breed.
Dad boasted about his artful bargaining, and how
He calmly escaped a peasant's anger over a prized
Animal. My brother Frantz beamed, showing off
His teeth for the grilled meat he dreamed of eating.
Gerald and I giggled, salivated at the thought
Of gobbling our own zesty chunks. Intoxicated
By the heat, we arrived at Saïra beach oblivious.

There, dad spoke to a local vendor, a large lady
In a navy blue dress, black headscarf tied beneath
Her straw hat, her hands swallowed by a black apron.
With a broad smile and a furtive head gesture, she sent
Two men to fetch the goat. We watched as if a present
Was being unwrapped. With a long pole threaded
Between the tied legs, they carried the dead animal
Upside-down. With just a tap on Gerald's shoulder,
We raced to the water's edge where soft waves greeted
Our bare feet. Not long after, we signaled
Underwater to each other as we counted seconds.

Breath racing, we scampered across the hot sand
To dad's table, by then surrounded by six plastic
Chairs and set underneath a small almond tree.
The sun had already begun to parch our skin
As we gawked at the large bowls filled with fried
Plantains, sweet potatoes, and crispy dark
Morsels of roasted goat. Hungry beach neighbors
Complimented dad for his stunning display.

As expected, dad prepared a large plate for each
Of their tables. We watched with dismay
As the mountain of meat dwindled into a hill.
I brought a plate to the table on our right, and Gerald
Went to the one to our left. The man who greeted me
Had a booming voice, and a basketball-sized belly.
With a broad smile, he sent dad one of his rum bottles.
The other neighbor sent fried fish, two big red snappers.
A marble-size lump descended down my throat.

I feared the winding road would turn into a two headed
Serpent, a nightmare on wheels as darkness would
Embrace our return. Dad traced my eyes, smiled,
Pushed the bottle, and signaled for us to eat.

Our fantasies turned us into chattering boys
With mouths full of dreams. We satiated ourselves,
Turning the roasted goat into the altar of our happiness.
When I noticed the bottle was barely touched,
Butterflies stopped fluttering in my chest,
And the goat's dead stare like stone gargoyles
Vacated the contour of my fear.

Miles of Remembrance, 1978

My pre-teen legs loved walking.
In elementary school, I once missed
The cherry red Daihatsu mini-van,
A Friday in April before the May holiday.

My mind ignored time as the football bounced
From ground to foot to rock-goal-posts,
Sea breeze to our left, onlookers clapping,
Screams of excitement drowned out Mr. Danbreville's horn.

Tall palm and coconut trees created an enclave
From the whirring cars on Harry Truman Boulevard.
We played until a penalty shot was called against our team,
time tricking me into dust, sweat and taut muscles.

My legs buckled under the weight of worries:
No pocket change, no extra bus fare,
No friends with a dime, and nine miles to tread.
With a biting hunger, I took my first steps home.

A mile down the road, out of lush grass and gated fences,
Parents with blond and rust-colored hair
Drove out of the Union School in Land-Rovers.
I envied their large, pristine campus, their American flag.

I longed to step in, but my Haitian tongue
Couldn't voice Shakespearean sounds. I walked on.
At the bend of the road, where the southwestern shore
Of Port-au-Prince Bay formed salty lagoons,

I watched flocks of pink flamingos, egrets and pelicans
Dotting the sea and looked past the miles ahead.
A grumbling gut urged me to hasten my steps
Soaked shirt, prickly feet for the distance yet travelled.

Tropical frescos on public buses with loud music,
Muscular porters framed my vision as sweat
Saturated my brow. I pushed on while the sun shifted,
Thinking of Grandpa with his stern gaze, raised eyebrows,

Hands clasped behind his back with a cowhide surprise.
As my feet nervously strode the last few yards toward
The house's gate, shouts of exultation rang out,
Followed by hard slaps for the grief caused.

I cried out of hunger. My dusted shoes
Became my makeshift odometer, each step
A memory opening like a morning glory,
Welcoming the monarch butterflies of my youth.

Neighbor's Garden

I gasped at my neighbor's garden—
pilfered seeds risen lush,
baskets swelling,
spilling their fruits.

Dad said, "do not
let history starve
behind one's door."
He pointed to the jutting bones
parading the streets.

I searched for paradise
but saw stripped mountains,
counted down to the elbowing hours,
needles of time stabbing famished ribs.

North Atlantic Circus

I was not introduced to the circus
as a child. North Atlantic magic
was projected through a two dimensional
TV, where jugglers rode on unicycles
and threw pins in rapid circles
as if they were four arms—Vishnu.

The universe spun in iron cages
with looping cyclists and daredevils
who rode their motorcycles sideways,
backwards, or standing as if riding
an iron horse. I swallowed those images
as natural as sacramental breads.

I was an adult, teaching
middle-school immigrants
when we encountered the circus.
Clowns jumping through flaming hoops,
and obedient elephants dropping
cake-sized dung, the air reeked.

We ate cotton candy and popcorn
while hoping the man and woman
balancing on a high-wired chair
in tight blue outfits
would not plunge the 30 feet

onto the un-netted painted floor.

So many images, so many whip-controlled tigers,
and growling lions executing tricks. A glittering
male trainer commanded with a metal wand
and a whip. Always a whip in this carnivalesque land.
Beneath the grunts, magic in the air. Cruelty stayed
behind the curtains with on-going applause.

Part Two

"The city is so vast
its ears have ceased to know
a simple human sound"
      —Edward Brathwaite
         ("The Emigrants"-*The Arrivants*)

Navigating

I-
It was never my dream to read the world,
Passing through clouds, leaving jet trails
Amidst gestures, languages, and leafing through
Pages in front of my eyes—Enchanted
Patchwork yet scared, unknown frailty.

Window seat, fading land, fading shore, fading sun.
New York, an ocean of lights, illuminated
A dark, menacing sky. I tasted the cold.
"Just come!" a group of Haitian cabbies hollered,
Guiding me back to the connecting terminal.

Traveling alone, my learnt English proved insufficient,
Misshapen words dispersed like seeds from my mouth:
"Hip me," instead of "help me." I hoped to end my journey
At the Port of Liberty, but a black woman from Philadelphia
Addressed me in French, ushered me to the Pan Am gate.

In Boston, I was greeted by my Bajan step-father,
His English a new tune to my ears. For a while,
Language rattled in my head. In Cambridge, the American
Dialect was speckled with Spanish, Amharic, Portuguese
And Jamaican patois. I cemented friendships with words.

II-
One day in early June, my mother shed tears as we idled
On Mass Ave, watching graduates enter Harvard Yard,
Wishing one of us would graduate from there.
It took me a while to understand Cambridge, its importance,
Its arrogance, as a town housing two colossal universities.

Two years later, I attended summer school there, studied with
A poet whose soft demeanor belied his experience. Vietnam on
His orange skin. With him, I discovered Martin Luther King's
Letter From Birmingham Jail. The bars of a divided United States
Weighed on my tongue as I grappled with a new understanding.

Rooted in Massachusetts, I discovered the Wampanoags,
Stripped of their hills and bays by trickery,
Decrees, smallpox, and bullets. I recognized the swords
And crosses of imposition and dispossession. The caravels
Brought diseases and despair since the first encounter.

In high school, I never met a Native American, but our mascot
Was an "Indian" head stamped on brown and gold jerseys. We
Were Warriors. I wore the lies of history. We shattered records.
My determined legs often first to cross finish lines; I became
Known as the Haitian sensation. From high school to college,

I found myself representing a people, a country handcuffed in despair.
Each step taken became an aspiration, a window to a world of dreams,
Shattered and rebuilt. Shattered again with piercing shards. I felt buried

In an open grave of excess, each consumption my flight on standby. I
Gasped for air, my eyes wandered the sky, gratte-ciel.

III-
I envisioned a horizon of palm trees, vertical swords gone
Weak like corroded nails. I wanted to take back my sky, but the cancer
Of corruption, indiscriminate bullets, and burning tires radiated into
The soil to ferment odium. Discouraged, I gave up track and the
Dream of wearing my nation's colors to an Olympic stadium.

I navigated into the republic of letters voicing my own anthem
With syllables that rejected nihilism and honeyed-tongues. I embraced
Césaire, Shengor, Komunyakaa, Bei Dao, Walcott, Pinsky, Laraque,
Espada and Heaney, running stanzas with. They're my mind-warriors
Stepping into a world doused in language and verve cadences.

Great doers of the word who hammered at pages, shaping my world.
Hands chiseling fat to bare muscles and bones, reflecting my own
Accent, my own tenor, so the lost Wampanoags could speak with
The Tainos, and Africans decomposed in the Atlantic crossing,
And those hacked on plantations where hatred was cultivated.

Having passed through many institutional doors, where Europe
Is affixed as the apex of knowledge, my dream is to re-read the world,
Leafing book pages where history isn't a blur of dove wings, but hands
Slapping natives into submission. Enchanted and no longer scared of
The discomfort of a barred tongue, I'll sing my anthem with an edge.

Windows of Exile

Wings soar in dawn's flares
uncovering the hidden aches of feet
treading slushy rivulets of snow.
The sun, a ripe orange
on the horizon, a mirage.
Wrapped heads and hands
remind tropical skins
this land is of fruit and thorns.

Knots torment my head, yearning
to hear the somersault of sea breezes.
In conch shells, the incision deepens,
loneliness carved by this savage winter.
Barren of heat and honeycombs, I seek
music to heal scars inflicted by an uncle
whose smile is a loaded M-16.

I dance anguished steps
when a man with unkempt hair
and cigar-stained teeth
chants "nigger" with a jaw
tightened like an unmerciful fist.
I wish to escape the rhythms of this land,
my words play different chords.

Tonight, although the sky is inviting,
deep blue, half lit,
stars gathering in clusters,
I stand behind my windows of exile
fanning my wings, waiting
for Haiti's spring to erase
the scorching heat from khaki uniforms,
and dragon eyes that pelt my native land.

Marooning

They've set their dreams sailing
toward the Windward Passage.
Hundreds packed on rafters
clinging to desires,
riding currents across the Atlantic,
trying to escape fishbone existence
and hawkish eyes.

In the night sky,
Toussaint's descendants maroon themselves
heading towards metallic Lady Liberty
with haggard hopes.
Once proud founders of freedom,
they are once more, children of salt,
avoiding sharks and coast-guard cutters,
cutting waves, cutting dreams.

Feet-damped, skull-baked.
They've set their dreams sailing
toward the Windward Passage.
Dark faces beaten by the sun,
and blistered hopes marked by scarlet stains,
refusing to be consumed by the whirlwind
of lurking death. They continue to navigate
Westward in search of Juan Ponce de Leon's

legends: Florida's water and gold.

Once ashore, they find neither the eternal fountain
of youth, nor riches. Instead, some land at Chrome
with their blistered hopes locked-up, or are found
lifeless on sandy beaches. Their corpses disturb
fenced-Greenbacks' eyes. Others slip their way
amongst Florida's downtrodden until they are
rescued by family members. Their daubed lives, Agwe,
the spirit of the sea, spared in the waves of life's
incisions where poverty, like Atlantic sharks,
awaits with rows of festive teeth.

Elegy For My Father

I was twenty when my father died.
I cursed the gods like a storm,
from Cambridge to Brooklyn.
His love was my barrier reef.
Life became a flashback of the heart.
Mom taught me how to stitch
my ripped pants and how to meet
with dad in secret, like they always did.
I remember one morning in 1970,
I was four, dressed in white shirt
and short khaki pants, holding my mother's
hand. She wore a hibiscus-printed dress.

My grandfather stood by the gate waving,
as my new ankle-high boots collected dust.
We walked to the bend in the road
until we reached the main street,
where my father's red jeep idled.
I never understood why mom and dad
met in secret, why their kisses and touch
could not cross Grandpa's eyes.

As the years curdled under my gaze,
I came to know that adults have secrets,
layers that cannot be peeled like

an onion. How foolish were my prayers
to the rosary beads when dad announced
his departure, and mom tasted the salt of mourning.

As I stood before my father's coffin,
crowned with flowers, my eyes surveyed his face,
peaceful, mouth sealed, eyes closed.
I thought I saw tears on his face, once more,
like when I was eight, his head resting
on my mother's shoulder, crying.
His brother, an uncle I never knew,
had died in Texas. I too cried.

Unexpected

It was early November 1986,
at night, the air had started to bite,
as if in the breath of an ugly dream,
words departed my mouth when my brother
Gerald called and said a nurse found dad
face down, by the window, empty of air.

A ram's horn punctured my lungs.
I panted until my face needed a raincoat.
Dad was only 56, and could no longer carry
his New York cross of stodgy air.
This city will never be the same again.
Its entrance, absent of his embrace, remained
a rainbow of neon in the soulless sky.

I pulled back the curtain of memory,
wishing I was sitting by the window,
brushing his hair back, the way he liked it,
and whispering my love before I drove back
up north, replaying my childhood:
the long drives we used to take to Léogane,
the aroma of crushed sugar cane
occupying our nostrils while dad inhaled
the scent. We would smile and then giggle.
Life seemed so sweet then, but we never knew

the harpoons he harbored.

Then, ten years after his death, he came knocking.
Wanting me to emerge from my internal bunkers.
Unexpected, I held my fountain pen and swam
inside my own innards to surface with memories
like sitting on a boulder, his arms around me, watching
the setting sun over the Atlantic ocean. I closed my eyes,
unlatched the evening, and felt reassembled, unshattered.

Echoes of Home, 1991

I wanted to rekindle my memories. My athletic
legs were eager to tread on the tarmac of memories.
After ten years of absence from my homeland,
more people, more cars, fewer trees—I was hesitant.

A saddened heart moaned inside of me. Tires
and abandoned cars strewn in rubbish-filled lagoons:
flamingos, egrets, and pelicans evicted. Slums
rose like a ratty army setting makeshift camps.

The scenery fragmented, viewed through
a shattered mirror, drunken vision.
I walked, unaware of my clenched fists, as my past
ran toward me with dead and truncated dreams.

The ocean seemed more distant, even foreign.
Cinder block houses turned their backs
to the shore, as chaotic paths led to doors
intoxicated on their hinges. Life has grown unhinged, bitter.

Harry Truman Boulevard had turned into potholes,
and junkyard parcels. The Union School shuffled its pupils
away from the multitudes and climbed to the shaded hills,
shard-guarded walls and gated communities. I walked on.

My grandpa's house, now sold. I strolled through my old
neighborhood incognito: goateed, capped, and sixty pounds
heavier. The boys' feet drummed against soccer balls—
a persistent ritual. I recognized some of the guys.

I walked on with a different beat to my steps, afraid my
old cadence would betray me. I gestured hello,
a customary nod, and cocked my ears for whispers.
No one knew the foreign body that walked on.

Rebirth
For Grandpa F.P.

I am dancing with faltering steps in a consuming
land of spiked honey. My flight to the carousel
of possibilities brought tears to my grandfather's
angry eyes. His ancestral land confiscated, stripped
and hauled for bauxite. Now, an eroded site.
an unknown great-uncle buried with lead in the guts.
What am I to do when my land grimaces
and the breath of hell propels people onto paper boats?

I have taken permanent residency
in a carnival land of possibilities
where hooded masquerades are celebrated
with fireworks. Burnt flesh in a photograph
hung in faded memories. Cotton, picked,
meshed, fabricated into white cloths
by Fulani and Hausa descendants, hung.
I am hanging in the salon of verses
where history shadows are translated
into pastoral stanzas, burying vocal couplets
that divulged the strange fruits of Southern poles:
poplar, popular, bulging eyes. Hanging.

I have taken permanent residency
in a land of orange agents clad

in Samish suits tailored for an Uncle
who wears a maniacal monocle.
His gaze envisions an ecosystem
of Stars and Stripes stripping roots
of robust mahoganies and cotton-silk wood
without stubborn fire brushes so progenies
could transform into Quasimodos
dreaming of winged-angels and celestial bells.

Hell, an ironclad lung for those whose spines
scaffolded the land. I closed my eyes
and dreamt of Moses reborn with the blood of Thor.
Possibility is the narrative of possibilities.
I caught the thunder's whims in a land of dreams.
My grandfather, buried with stubborn eyes,
never read my lines, compressed in the mind's crevices.

I flew on a metallic eagle's wings with fears
tucked into a blue suitcase. No regrets, just
the trepidation of time and tales of violence
cleaving capricious hopes. My mother, counting time
to re-unite, secretly seeded a new crop into
my unquiet heart. She did not know that the vestiges
of memories would converge into verses, a new genesis.

I flew into a carnival land of possibilities
and took permanent residency with parchment,
so memories like collagen can melt onto surfaces.

I embrace the noesis of my mother's dreams.
My grandfather's bones are dust, despite residues,
his gaze still locked upon my steps I spun onto
the carousel, a go-round that can make merry,
or regurgitate certain syntaxes into oblivion.

New York, NY

Sidewalk poets with razor-wire tongues
lash truths like whirling dervishes.

Workers, dealers, traders, hookers—
silence, chewing their lunch.

The city is a nightmare; rocket skylines
thrust hard against a phantom sky.

Pollution veils the angels' eyes,
while sidewalk poets inhale obscenities.

They teeter at the edge,
twisted lines for lives.

The apple tastes of rot. Truth and clean air
are as rare as sycamores in Manhattan.

And yet, beneath the subways, voices spark—
molten syllables forging their own constellations.

Denial
For all EDPs

In the middle of
a blistering,
bone-chilling winter,
colonized toes
sing requiems
inside French
or Italian shoes.
Their metered steps
measure
the bitterness of exile,
while dreams
merge with the
scarred blotches
on calendars.

Existing

In the cardinal points of belonging,
royal robes draped over the Atlantic,
archipelagoes reduced to aristocratic undergarments.
Slovenly calicos for field hands
laboring in the tropics.

In the cardinal points of belonging,
tongues waxed to mirror dominion's dictum.
French, a lingua franca of guilt.
Polished mouths estranged from kinship,
over-enunciating exile.

In the cardinal points of belonging,
skins French-fried in plantation skillets.
Millions seasoned, sizzled, nouns drowned
in cauldrons. Molasses lacquered descendants' tongues,
too heavy to lift the unforgiving "U".

Naked in the cardinal points of belonging,
conquest remains a violent intimacy.
Fragmented beings praised beneath the Eiffel Tower,
forgetting the grammars of humiliation,
the syllabi of plantations, nations drowned.

In the cardinal points of belonging,

machetes and swords swung dominion's decree.
But the scarlet of royal robes bled only furry.
Garroting autonomy,
millions endure with stammering tongues.

Semblance

I had fallen into a camouflaged landscape,
as quicksand filled my marital marrow.
No one captured the first injuries: a grain of sand
in the eye, blurred frame, mortified portraiture.
Keeping silent was no longer an art.
Hostilities became neatly packaged snapshots.

My gaze, fixated upon octagonal angles,
was ensnared in a web of lust. I drifted
through a fragile façade until irritation
flickered and flared. Smiles faded, distant
as the crescent moon. We hollered,
our echoes ricocheting off plastered walls.

After many bouts of words hurled
like daggers against plastered walls,
I realized there was a labyrinth of syntaxes
in her speech. I collapsed to the floor,
the shaggy carpet soaking up my tears,
a silent spectator to my unraveling.

I couldn't walk away from my shadow.
I felt glued; flesh stuck to bones, an unwanted
self. My blood pumped nightmares.
Choked air, fleas fled sleep.

The house was a univocal universe.

Contained, I yearned to escape the floor's embrace.
Light for my weight, I delved underground,
seeking solace in Monk's melody.
I slid into the CD player, nestling
beneath Monk's right shoe. He kicked,
stepped, and braked; his fingers danced

across black and white keys, creating "Ugly Beauty."
Ejected from the scene, the floor welcomed
me back, the carpet dry. But her mouth
persisted, flashing like a firefly in the dark.

Searing Daggers

I was not born under a confined sky.
Despite nightsticks and door beatings,
torrential downpours have pounded my shoulders.
Ducking and covering is an art
in times of war.
I learned to dodge your daggers,
hiding behind hardcovers,
my armor against your hatchets.

Your wrath can no longer steamroll
me into a trampling sod mat.
Your landscape of malevolence
is enclosed with venomous mortar, with which
you construct a perilous anthill. Inside,
a gullible son douses his splendor.

Our child languishes in the anthill,
he has not discovered a refuge in books,
and raindrops do not sluice down his
back. Your traps have snagged his legs,
searing his steps like the burned
groove of my left hand.

I wish I had known you were
kerosene. Haitian-born under Duvalier,

Belgium-educated under King Leopold.
Your roads were carved by spikes and spite,
charred malaise, tarred.
How gullible were my eyes?
Your first nuptial ended with the groom
drowned in scotch. You were a walking
Scotch bonnet.

Epidermopolis

My skin is paper-thin,
and your tongue the secateurs
that hack the harmony
of beings. You place pinks
above all primary colors and call
your new hierarchy a reconstruction.

My skin is paper-thin,
and your reconstruction
is wrapped in tin foil promises,
letters disintegrating under
the heat of neo-Jacksonian jackboots.
Chain gang hums pulsate on my skin;
I shuffle with my cancerous future.

My paper-thin skin has been slashed,
marked, and striped with bindings
that clutch hands in burlap. Oh saints!
You refuse to hear the notes that begged
for my dead skin. I'm skinned alive
while the bugle mutes my cries.

My skin is a specter, this organic thin sheet
has caused men to adorn sheets,
to smooth communication with angry ghosts

whose estates were large plantations. Perhaps
they're missing the whips that sang on skin,
making cotton southern snow. Field ghosts
flake on ashy skin. I choke on history.

A Night in Brooklyn
For Abner Louima

In the pre-dawn of humid August heat,
lovers and strangers danced slowly
on an unbuffed wooden floor. Bodies
tightly held, defying light in the dim room.
Hands embraced backs, buttocks.
Someone got jealous, grabbed,
or slapped somebody else's lover.
A brawl broke out, no guns, just swinging fists.

The music stopped, panic-filled screams
boomeranged. A hand dialed 911.
Puffing officers in dark blue,
stormed through Rendezvous Night Club,
where Haitian immigrants gathered
to dance under Phantom's honey-thick
tropical rhythm. Black backs met
discriminating billy clubs frantically swinging.

More officers rushed out of wailing cars,
brandishing Nines and shotguns. Brooklyn's
Flatbush Avenue became intoxicated
by the frenzied footsteps of the city's
Gestapos with rhinoceros-like strength.
Even the saints stopped marching to gather

their unshed tears in prayer. A unit
of stars streaked by, wailing.

When Abner Louima, a thin, dark-skinned
security guard, tried to reason, his ribs were greeted
with breath-stopping jabs. Handcuffed, head-locked,
canopies of black migrant bodies, canned.
Blood-stained, had Abner known the reputation
of badged-uniforms, he would have avoided Officer
Volpe the way he sidestepped Duvalier's bogeymen—
dream predators, ecstased by others' torment.

Behind the prison wall of a Brooklyn precinct,
Volpe concocted a sadistic game of Sodomy.
Inebriated by frenzied rhythms of kicks and
punches, freedom waited with an axe.
They danced around his limp molested body,
Abner's dignity flushed in a polyrhythm of groans.
His life hung on a thread of luck, threads,
hundreds of yards to stitch him back to life.

History of Laments

The ocean twitches in limbs,
cuts loose shipwrecks in our veins.
Millions entombed,
their chain links clattering through history.
And we cruise the Atlantic, island hopping—
it is not the jangle of the chains,
but the lives scattered, clustered in constellations
across a bleeding continent.

Work angels linked
to lines of unending fluencies, nourishing
towers of sphere-influence. Algorithms
brace skyscrapers where gold
and diamonds ignite desires of Ponziers.

I sheathe myself with the memories of the
Choctaw, Tainos, Arawaks, and Yorubas—
morphing my abode into a swift bayonet
of a temple. Our backs cannot remain
a coveted trampoline—lives trampled
for centuries, absent of conscience.
Now silence prevails, as if the past were vaulted
in the void: unspeakable domes of bones.

Regardless of bible-thumping and trumpet-blaring
for a blessed providence, we hear the corroding chains.
Skeletons framed structures of success; crossbeams,
memories forming transversal recollections.
The genesis of your market, Wall Street,
is imprinted on our sugar-crushed backs.

A bricolage of dead dreams
rests at the bottom of the Atlantic.

I try to stitch patches of poetry from ancestral tongues,
refusing to expose their succumbed brutalities.
I am committed to un-scab the past with a fountain pen,
until Atlantic's water spirits lament
in harmonic, disemboweled wails.

Canonized Token

Remember, you are not of the canon.
Powder your tongue to be known,
and tread lightly on wooden planks,
for splinters can destabilize a swagger.
Admire the halls with a blithe smile,
swallow your edgy adjectives with grace.
At the tabernacle, be proud
to display your canonized verbiage—
a local oddity.
You will be embraced,
placed on a bantam altar,
a token with a swagger.

Blue Blood

I am a biped moving beyond silence,
straining a meager existence in the mind's
foliage. Crafting a collage of syntax
that names the breathing world of my skin.

Highbrow vocabularies cannot be used.
Here, tongues wax blue blood.
Oh! Cowboys still blaze the world with a simple
word: freedom. Horrors yet undone, unspoken.

What is free about feeding the air acid
and dumping nuclear waste onto countries
where skins do not reflect the snow? Cold.
I care not for concave and buffed sentiments.

I bite with multisyllabic bats—chasing vampires
of empires—straight, no chaser while-shuffling.
The world grieves from simple utterances,
waterboarding. I gag from an inventory of rags.

Cowboys fling dictators across jungle-thick skies
where natives are unarmed storytellers.
Blue blood gained from chained labor,
my umbilical cord still linked to Cain's canes.

Part Three

"Don't pretend to be sleeping,
remember your troubadour;
for I now understand…understand
the human equation of your love."
      _César Vallejo
            ("Rain"-*The Completed Poetry)*

The Coffin Maker & The Poet

For Jacques Roche

Together:
We are from a flogging island
Where gusting winds turn dreams
Into dust and tattered houses kneel
Upon rocky hills, imploring
The desolate land. Tomb-like
Abodes stud the city, and nailing
Shut disfigured dreams.
As tyrannical waves flog the island,
We hope for an affable rhythm.

Coffin Maker:
I've watched you perambulate
With confident steps and wondered about
Your height. I want your dreams to repose
Within a receptacle made of cedar and pine.
You are a peacock in your bearing,
And your exit from this land must pass
Through my workshop. Splendid and
Crafted, witnessed by the nostalgic.
But if I depart first, pen me a poem.

The Poet:
I've walked by your shop, drawn to
Fresh scent of poplar, pine & cedar.
The whirring music of your saws hum
To my probing ears. I wonder about the dead trees.
Our mountains are barren; our lives romped
By the riotous orgy of disorder, a macabre dance

Burying hopes in coffin coffers. Ominous hearses,
Funeral-carnivals clamor in the streets.
You have grown muscular from sawing
Trees that beg not to be turned into coffins.

Coffin Maker:
Poet dreamer, you walk among trees
And do you not pen your poems on flesh?
The trees too cried as they turned into paper.
Perhaps the shark-like teeth of my chisel
And whirring sounds of iron slicing through
Wood bleed ears, but your pen is
A blade too. Sharp, unforgiving, a social dagger.
Some in this city burn under your pen's fire
Refusing to fix their out-of-step dance,
Your piquant lines are the peoples' tunes.

The Poet:
We are the people my friend. You build
Our wooden boxes of permanent dormancy;
I scribble the whaling sounds of the land
That burn my pen into an amber metal,
Glowing on our charred roads. Ravaged
Memories implode in the trappings of needs.
Time is unforgiving in this cramped island
Where blood-binging tyrants make the coffin
Makers consume more trees than poets.
Your sawdust will not obstruct my voice.

Coffin Maker:
My sawdust will not filch the beaming aura
Of your gaze, nor suffuse the morning dew
Of your voice. You must recite your poem
About the dog that gulped poverty while dreaming

Of his old broth plate. We escape through your words,
And our eardrums make us dance to your rhythm.
Swaying as if in a meditative state, we hang to the edges
Of your words. In this terrestrial darkness
You are a sunbeam and no dust can cloud your light.

The Poet:
I dreamt I was swaddled in one of your coffins.
Mourners gathered in front of your shop like
A chapel. Twisted cotton meshes burned
In orange-peel halves filled with palm oil,
As mass was said by a disfigured priest holding
A black book. He took elliptical breaths between
The lines, disrupting the cadences. Fire sputtered
Through eyes carving my name on lacquered
Cedar. Our crying forest has been ditched by tyrannical
Waves. Hacked planks beg in this saw-buzzing kingdom.

Coffin Maker:
In this kingdom, this barren land of bones, convulsion
Is the rhythm. Dust gags dreams. Rags gag poets.
Crying becomes ritual as poetry is to eulogy,
And coffins are to funerals. I chisel my art on coffers
of last rites, a planetarium of one's own, so dignity,
The last possession can be protected from maggots.
I apologize for the trees, but death is the rhythm
Of tyrants and its racket pervades disconsolate borders.
Lives are unhinged doors and broken twigs. Soundproof
Coffins are sealants for gutted and mutilated humanities.

The Poet:
In a kingdom of chaos where rocks and bullets are
Shooting stars, the poet's pen is not the magic wand
That will stop the eternal unraveling of lives. I've tried

To pen dreams into structures, but my ink bled. This
Is the avalanche of despair where ribs crack as twigs
Under the weight of boots. Broken, unhinged, crumpled.
In this terrestrial darkness, my friend, you bequeathed
Me a sunbeam and now no dust can cloud my light. I am
The moving target of advancing dictators. I fear my dreams.
Newly constructed doors become stretchers. Bloodied,
Cadavers pass through crowded streets without sirens.

Together:
We are from a flogging island where gusting winds
Turn dreams into dust and tattered houses kneel
Upon rocky hills, imploring the desolate land.
Tomb-like abodes stud the city, nailing shut
Disfigured dreams. As tyrannical waves flog the island,
Like whales, we moan for this land.

Coffin Maker:
In the shadow of a moonless July night, a star was netted,
Chained and handcuffed to a chair. We waited four days
In the dark until we knew your eyes would no longer reflect
The sun. My poet friend, my orbit is now unbalanced
In this chaotic kingdom. They left you without
Your rhythmical tongue and shackled you with a rusted chain.
Your hand swelled behind your back as you were dumped
Shirtless and shoeless on the hot pavement. Your blue
Shorts glistened beside a pool, as an island of blood
Trailed from your head. The earth convulsed.

Contumelious
for Nicolas Chauvin

I walk into a world dreaming
of blue jays and turtledoves.
A mischievous hand plucks a feather
from my wing, I squawk like a hawk.
Chauvin becomes my travelling companion.

In pain, I totter to the plaza,
where a white-gloved hand
hurls speaking scorpions at me.
My ancestors taught me the power of honey.
I drip golden drops on their claws,
an army of red ants pierces their shells.

I carry syllables of ghosts,
names of soldiers from far continents,
prefixes, suffixes, and whole sentences
attached to my name.
I'm never alone in the crossroads of words.
I climb the tower of Babel;
a constrictor contuses my corpus,
Chauvin etches on my chest.

The wind in Academe shifts, I hurry for safety.
Cracked mouths beg for water
in the queen's courtyard.
With jeweled hands she offers a solitary rose,
long-stemmed and prickly. My fingers bleed a regiment.
Toussaint walks with Chauvin,
and all the horses neigh in excitement.

As I cross the yard of knowledge,
rose petals sink into mud.
Drunken scholars dance with their own words,
I, a black corpse tied with guitar strings.
They chant ancient anthems to the crickets' philosophers.
I feel unsafe with Chauvin as my travelling companion.

I scrub my chest before the mirror.
Chauvin stands guard in a pristine Napoleonic uniform,
smirking. His name brands my corpus.
I become a tempestuous legionnaire,
testifying against my own masculinity.
Wounded, I wobble in Academe's desert,
where exhaustion builds mirages.

I bar the balcony of my ears
so the queen's venomous words
cannot linger in me.
I walk through the crossroads of speared logos
with a spine like a royal palm—
dignified. I sever Chauvin's strings.

My father transcended terra cognita
some fifteen years earlier, handed me a dictionary.
His words return as a reminder:
"Poets dissect the world with similes,
and prescribe metaphors." From beyond he shreds
Chauvin, unseats the queen, and whispers in my ear
the way mothers sing their babies to sleep.

Benedictus

I am skeptical
of professors who preen
before gilded mirrors
of enlightenment.
Weary, too, of preachers
who commune with the Holy Ghost,
perhaps no more than drunkards
who find Jesus at the bottom
of fermented spirits.
Yet, I am fond
of zombies
who wear crowns of thorns.

Logos

My poems are too political, you say as you place
a slice of Gouda onto your mouth. A pause,
then a sip of Malbec while you eye me
for an answer. I chew my words, too spicy for
your ears, and let out a bored cat grin to ease
the map of anxiety flashes on your ocular yoke.

I'm homo historicus, I reply. I live in a metropolis.
I cannot subtract polis from metro, nor can I add
bougainvilleas and marigolds to the islands that were
seized by Prospero and inherited by his progenies.
I've learned the language taught to Caliban, and
no art can plague my tongue. No Ariel can veil
my eyes, or slumber me to a land of wonder.

Comrade, your honey-glazed existence will lead
to diabetes. May I suggest leaving the honeycomb
for a long durée promenade upon rocky shores to survey
the empty shells, the crushed eggs, the twisted necks
of red-tailed tropicbirds, and thresher sharks
that maraud the coasts. Then, let's write a poem
together where logos are uninhibited like the wind.

Congestion

The city of my birth is drowned
with drunken footsteps spattering
their existence in clumps of flames.
Barrage of hunger and anger tearing

in the fuselage of benevolence. We fly
on fear, parking streets with caskets
begging for compassions as commerce
fortified their inertia raining distress.

Lives congested in rows of poverty,
snarled progress to a century of hoes
and machetes where tattered selves
cried laughingly at gated gates gazing

coldly. The city of my birth is drowned
in fear of the impoverished, deprived
of the iota of being. Life is congested,
infested with beings dying to be beings.

Their insolvent bodies lined heartless
municipalities congested with greased
palms. Mollusk politicians haughtily volute
themselves under the footstools of moguls.

Convulsion

Darkness resonated beyond the coastline
pulsating in waves releasing moanful
rhythms as battered bodies set adrift
on the ocean, desperate and tattered.

Paradise is a shipwreck of eternity
with waves of survivors convulsing
sugarcane blues into the sacristies
of militarized vaults. We are cramped

in chaos. Debris of the past piled into
ensembles where dreams are trapped
in the threshold of heavens, clasped
hands plagued by buoyant assonance

clapped until wrecked beneath the stars.
Hard-won happiness returned to darkness
as melancholy treacherously scuttled
throughout the island in paroxysm waves.

Just at the seaside, generations of children
moaned the ingested splinters from the
Santa-Maria and markets encrusted sugarcanes
that pressed the buoyancy of souls into pulp.

Centuries of Ashes

The shard-like fury of Port-au-Prince
will slice through social veins
and harvest life with a machete.

Hungry and crowded streets
will be lit with flamboyant trees,
flowering the redness of anger.

Two centuries of ashes and blind privilege
hoarding in palaces, suffusing fetidness
with extraneous air-fresheners.

Two centuries of ashes and cruelty
have been mastered with a surgeon's
precision. We laugh as we bleed.

Despite drunken drums
and frolicsome hips,
shard-like anger will rankle,

streaming through peasant fields,
shanty towns and regal abodes the way
red ants march on pressed sugarcanes.

Despite drunken drums and frolicsome hips,
drifting angels will wing themselves away
the way bats flock out of dark caves.

Cocoon of Poverty

For P. Laraque, N. Roc & in memory of J. Roche

When words flap and jab in my chest,
my metered compass is nudged to the line.
My nation is a caterpillar clawing
against the cocoon of poverty.
I watch with guttered mouth, flaming eyes.

Bullets flare against my swollen lids.
A wounded nation writhes, starved and raw.
Death-angels circle the moaning mountains.
Prostitute-politicians crawl on their knees,
tongues greased with Atlantic spit,
palms stretched wide for scraps.
My mouth is a rain-gutter.

In the center of my chest,
where the rain has pooled,
muffled words throb and crowd
like caged doves cooing unmet desires.
Clouds wander this mortal corpus,
so poetry will not cease to grieve a nation.

We were seared by molasses, scarred by the tropic's cancer,
while green eyes—gluttonous for coffee and cacao—
bent the mountains to our backs.
We have become backward and destitute.

My cheeks burn as drenched eyes turn seaward.
Thousands of paper boats drifting west.
Underwater bodies become vessels,

laden with conches and bells that toll the wind
to grant us passage, so we may return with flowers
to our carrion-birthplace.

Boulevard Jean Jacques Dessalines

Again, I've been insulted at the common market.
July, Boulevard Dessalines reeking with human
Sweat, burnt oil and a carnival of shouting vendors.
I captured images onto magnetic tapes.
Frenzied hands tugging used American blue jeans,
Weary feet slipping into used leather shoes.
I shouldered my camera steadily as rivers of sweat
Streamed past beaming yellow eyes.

Jean Jacques Dessalines has gathered his chopped
Remains and remounted his horse. Vexed
By the polluted soil and dingy urchins begging
Underneath broken storefronts. Dessalines Boulevard
Is a chaotic heap where hips violently sway
To navigate busied feet that rid of goods so children
Will not go hungry. I zoomed in on frenzied hands,
Grabbing worn foreign goods. I panned and framed
Pouting lips, a desperate buyer noticed my invading lens.
Our misery is a splintered cross with protruding nails.

July, as my memory chokes on dust and filth,
I finally dare to write down what I witnessed
On Jean Jacques Dessalines Boulevard.
Port-au-Prince has been assassinated,
Cut into wanton pieces waiting to be buried
Underneath a universe of garbage. I can't erase
The carnival of vendors with their cacophonous
Sounds and lurid gazes, nor the fat woman
In a deep purple dress sweating, spread-legged,
Wearing a fake gold chain around her thick black neck
As she meticulously places bundles
Of dirty Gourdes into her brassiere.

A Palace of Mourners

I sought to cage memories,
Houdinis escaping
from opaque brain cells harboring
a palace of mourners. In my birth country,
nightsticks swung from Columbus
to modern leaders, fear simmered
and poured into our veins.

After nights of needles pricking my sleep,
floods of images breached the dam of silence.
Joseph, a twenty-six-year-old journalist
arrested in August of '92, demanded to speak.
My skull became an echo chamber
where the dead reverberated—
their screams shattering corrals of memory,
their tapestry woven with Joseph's blistered back,
his broken knee, cicatrized head.

The army wanted to teach him
the grammar of silence.
Thin wires glowed,
turned his tongue into an eel,
slapping words into nonsense.
Still, he would not bow or confess.
He trumpeted justice through scars,
through the body's refusal to obey.

Even with this carnival of nightsticks
and stench, I tried to write
of clouds, of pastoral stillness.

But screams of a valley of Haitians
migrated ferociously across my page,
tearing lilies and dandelions to shreds.
On the palace lawn, no flowers remain—
only the bald eagle's wings spread wide.

Grieving

We uncovered a basin of stone graves
on the outskirts of a cane plantation,
we silently grieved inside blank pages.
Steady hands once scribed the sizes of shackles,
leafy scrolls cried the pain of a rebellious people.
Still paying for ancestral battalions
that escaped festive portals of lashes.

Now, we are a scattered vineyard of bones
engulfed by the promise of joyful rain,
but the sweltering sun squelches dreams.
We are without a Moses, without homes.
As centuries of hate crystallize pain
in our beings, we soldier on to fletch.

Prolongation

Clouds of dust mushroomed the city
With every tumbling, crumpled block,
Bearing semblance to Hiroshima.
Cities of ruins, of agonies, of broken bones.

The air sordidly pregnant with corpses
Wore necklaces of flies, saint-less.
A hell of sewage overflowed in the temple
Of existence as the hacked capital cracked.

Lives lacerated by a lack of civility, a gluttony
Of buttressed egos, je ne sais quoi. Charlatans
From the country of L'Ouverture, in cahoots with barons
Of the chained world. Salt and sugar merchants.

What existence can be lived on peanut wages?
Lives morphed inside cocoons of poverty cannot become
Butterflies, only debased caterpillars condemned to crawling
Among the rubbish of catatonic deprecations.

With every tumbling and crumpling block,
A nation denigrated its existence by nailing
Contempt to those whose navels pumped marrow
Into the dorms of opulence and extravagance:

Marseilles, Versailles, Brussels, Luxembourg,
New York, London, Charlotte, Madrid, Liverpool,
And the nightmares coffered on Wall Street
Blow our existence into cavernous dust.

Cracked
For the IDPs

You sat pristine and impervious,
egg white shades on the crusting margin
of the sweltering tropical slum, hoping
your planetarium of mysterious hand shakes
will prevent the impulse of light from penetrating
chilled heartbeat chambers and pulsar of might.

Waves of hungry orphans crashed through your gates.
Sheathed by armored tanks, you brushed dust off your coat.
Renewed and protected, trepanned windows
stifled their voices.
Still, hands repeated century-old gestures
behind rugged mahogany desks and marble floors.

In the impious world of umpires, empires are never
eternal. Not you, although you were inhabited by
two emperors, you never made it into the digest of empires,
but you've been digested and regurgitated like wild grass
in a cow's entrails; trailing misery to the forefront
of the manicured lawn and fenced water-sprinklers.

If you knew the penance that awaited you
on that sweltering January, you would have asked
for better housekeepers, and guests of honors.
Thirty rumbling seconds broke your pristine
shells and slumming you to the un-pastoral bughouse
that cancroid your presence on the stately manicured lawn.
Millions of bodies are now camped at your knees.

Stripped and cracked, you are now a planetarium. Kneeling
beggars and lights traversing through pulsing chambers
revealed the purse's might, as hungry orphans' hands dialed
the old chambers of empires for relief and consolation.
Ancestral victories once colossal, are shriveled memories,
as your cracked column morphed into a stooping vertebrae.

Haiti: A Disavowal

Home, the center of intimacy is wilting in its solidity.
Am I fooling myself by shedding tears for that land rocked
By turbulence, where perched cardinals go on feeding
As eagles and other rapacious birds claw through sparrows'
Nests as if their existence was pure dispensable meat?

My enemies have shown themselves. Friends, beasts
With corporate smiles constantly slashing handshakes
For sugar, cacao as if nature is not fierce enough. Lunacy.
The lunatics are behind glass walls howling like wolves
For the pearl of the moon. The sparrows already consumed.

I feel naked, breached by hate for my nocturnal skin
As names, affixed to a collective, became settlements.
When my feathers are plucked, the bayonet of my beak
Knows the history of steel, clacking, and gashing through
Flesh avowing dignity. Centuries of my disavowed liberty.

The blood of my ancestors is no longer in the marrow,
And cardinal concords are signed where lives latched to capital
Exist on the margins with the stench of skins drenched
In centuries of field labor. Drudgers in tatters eating dust.
Under the eagle's claw, home is a nest of dead sparrows.

We've been on our knees since the viperous cross was planted,
And I stood naked beneath an oak's mistletoe, genuflecting.
No white bulls, no white cloak—only my blackness bonding
With the moon. A choir versed the nation of the heart:
Home, the intimate abode, though cardinals are not sanguine.

My birthplace is an irritant; its cardinals are moles.
Liberty aborted—Louverturean sparrows eaten by wolves.
I have no drinking horns, but my lunar pendant is a gift
From Sulis Minerva, descendant of the Black Madonna.
Madre de la tierra, I am earth of the earth; my inheritance,
earth.

Confluence

Between us, there were never any hallucinations.
In the firmament of our destiny, iridescent haloes
bridged our unity. We boarded a ferry
leaving behind bitterly crusted hearts.

Our inadvertent encounter became
an immaculate capturing of our souls,
streaming to a placid cove of rebirth.
Life chimed in with spellbound connections.

At the wee hour of despair, our hearts sought
solace in rays where cosmic tears propelled
my fortified being to reveal its structures,
and you unveiled your innermost sanctity.

The anatomy of words bound by flesh,
we began to construct with a surgeon's
precision, as hopes reconstructed particles
of our hearts. Turbulent past quieted.

We transformed each other's double helices.
Valves with red blood cells shot up
with plasma-perfect similitude of our beings.
Awaited offspring's arrival solidified our berth.

Menelik

At 4:00 p.m. that October you were extracted
wailing into light from a balled posture
with tightened fists, right arm extended,
and the left tucked firmly to your side.
A fighting stance. Muscular, you entered
this world determined not to be expelled
by the subserosal fibroids that prevented
your sister from growing to term.
From burning tears to gleeful tears,
you gave us our singing throats.
That first night, I sang you
To sleep as mommy hummed her pain
to her own sleep. You, blood of our blood,
an ocean of ancestral plasma swimming
through your veins, were made taut:
no ataxia, no angioplasty. Just wailing
that kept us from sleep. You are as
commanding as your namesake.
Your eyes knowing, lucid,
a star on the altar of our unhappiness.

Secret of La Sirène
For the water spirits

Five brown fingers grip each side of the sink
like tarantulas awaiting prey.
Gaped mouth, spine stooped.
Violent waves churn inside my stomach
discharging disagreeable legumes.
I hear forks clinking against plates,
and interspersed between laughter are the rolling
Waves of Negril where Reggae skank down worries.
A flash, fog forms in the bathroom.
I am in between worlds.
Who is this glazed-eyed man in the mirror?
I splash water on my face, trying to steady my gaze
as your figure, swathed in blue silk, floats across
the dome of my imagination. I thought.
You touch the suture on my left shoulder
the way a fairy would revive dead flowers.
My existence is in your sanctity.
You, shape-shifter, mother of all realms
no imagination could have produced the soft,
and yet piercing pitch of your voice:
"Invisibility is a way of migrating," you said.
I almost piss in my white linen pants.
Our sacred covenant was sealed before my birth;
you hemmed yourself into my christening gown
to purify the ablutions of Christianity.
Water is your abode, La Sirène, the element of life:
you bond, you brake, you transform,
but you always maintain. You've maintained
me in the archipelago of survival

where swords and machine guns
force spines to sow crops for citizens
of a street walled off to us. Tonight,
you prevented the food poisoning from lodging
into my system. Re-booted and refreshed,
I walk back into the enlivened dining room, erected
and knowing that I am rooted with my own siren.

Jujubean
For J. LB

With gritted teeth and chili pepper-eyes, you watched
My boat of desire sail into the horizontal abyss
As your heart pumped sorrow in its own harbor.

What you harbor toward me is an iron oar, cutting.
But our distance is an ocean of silence, and no number
Of oarlocks can clamp me back to your shore.

Years of cavernous pain, a grotto of guilt inside
My skull. How could I go on not penning a mea culpa?
You were once the essence, never cheap sex. A Blue Jay

Beyond the gift of beauty. You wanted the bonding of rings,
the cradling of heirs. I was too young for husbandry.
You trusted providence; sortilege was wrecking a good love.

I cannot kneel before you, siphon the pus of grief that
Festers your heart, but I can script my regrets into verse
For the song unsung upon the altar of "everlasting."

We heard the angels sing, and we intoxicated ourselves
With laughter (I remember, you loved cherry Pinot Noir).
But, you were too thin-skinned for my taste.

Instead, my hastened departure, like a rough seaman,
Brought waves of suffering onto your flawless coastline.
I was the first to have taken you to the rough seas.

You wanted for us to remain a tight cluster:

Conico-cylindrical, voluptuous, like the pinot grapes
You loved. That would have been a viticultural hazard.

Polarization

I am re-entering the past through constricted valves,
Memories of heavy palpitations that rushed me
To my physician's office, then to the cardiac unit.
I was wired. Thorough auscultation; strong heart,
Surpassing my male cohort, but the constriction was
Like a Buddha planted on my chest had sprung from
The stubborn divide that persisted between us. After
Our teeth-grinding divorce, you swore to terminate me,
And I vowed to remain unbroken. With each blow,
Tears morphed into poetry, my unbending spine
Became a target for your vile plots. I bolted down.

Fourteen years after our separation, we still meet in courts.
Split-tongued men in shark suits argued their own interests;
I watched purgatory through your gaze and wondered
If it would have been better to slowly bleed my happiness
Away through a sustained marriage, or endure ceaseless
Proceedings that incised misery into my being. Although
Tattered, I remained a bamboo, knowing that if the brackish
Water of your existence merged into my pond it would
Dissolve my marsh. With new spring rain, the island
Of our flesh became a speck of regrets.

Theseus' Shield

When fire ignites the soul, neither Daedalus'
minotaur, nor the Marathonian bulls
could slay the shielded Theseus. In the April
labyrinth of violence on Boylston, bodies were
sheathed by hands-like-wands untangling limbs.

Minos and Asterion weighed bones on
scales of framed power blustering pride.
A child fell from the sky, shattered.
Nightingales swallowed their fears and whimpered
requiems for an assaulted ground.

Inorganic cumulus clouds imbibed
a phantom army of ventriloquists
were ecstatic by ghostly mayhem,
but armored souls shielded by Theseus
became new stirring flames of affection.

Wings severed from herons flew with
memories of lineage, cells of yesteryears.
Amidst flowers, placards and trinkets,
Lazarus roamed the roads as taxon
without the hope of resurrection.

A town gripped by grief shuffled away

from shards and shattered dreams toward
gates of liquid faith where communion
armored souls with a new grammar of hope.
Boston's sorrows are tucked under bold prints.

Underworld Enterprise

Inside the orange jumpsuit is a great-grandfather,
a frail body that harbors unfathomable harm.
I first encountered your name on the streets
without knowing the height of Winter Hill.
Today, you are my muse as I scribble
in a black notebook over a countertop.
Through large storm windows, I watch
the nakedness of Eastern hemlock
and sycamore, leaves strewn in the streets.

I wonder what you think of African
elephants, the poaching of tusks
for the money you lust after?
I imagine you, around a dim-lit harbor,
calmly inspecting crates of ivory as your crew
cashes-in from the slaughter of families.
Elephants, rhinos, humans…
To you, consciousness is pollution.

Somehow, you are next to me, both in print
and in the softness of the afternoon light,
my eyes trace the pen's shadow.
Exposed obscurities.
Remembrance of a father, a life parted
at the end of a gun. Crotches threatened,

heads butted, and bodies mutilated in shallow graves.
In these parts of town, ink spilled about you.
You are fear and mythology.

Someone calls you a vainglorious bigot
and a Neanderthal. You remain silent,
knowing where blacks and women belong.
Your supremacy allowed you to bruise the world.
Flesh trafficking is just transaction.
I am looking at your thinning white hair horseshoed
around a red scalp, where unspeakable mayhem
are buried beneath your bifocals. White bushy
eyebrows, terse lips, you've become a silent spectacle.

You've grown in the belly of barrels, where capital
is the fire of sustenance: a vile that feeds gluttony
like wood fire. Through the nozzle, you learned
to lengthen your roots as your climbing vines
twisted into resisting arteries. Parts of the city
bulged by the girth of your roots, a sorrow
draining families onto despair. You became
the pipeline, the smear on the setting sun.
A gunslinger, son of a gun.

Now, grieving hearts eagerly await
the iron cell that will contain your lungs.
All the poaching for the trophy of ivories,
the sharpness of the butchering knife,

maybe the precision of the guns.
Now silence. Still,
thousands of lives concealed under slabs.

Lost in silence, you furrowed your brow
as voices wept, seeking to enter your mind's eye
and drift to retrievable memories,
but un-retrievable lives. This is your last shot
in the limelight. Someone in Beantown burns
with desire to see you pulverized
like detached elephant tusks.
You shuffle into silence.

Thirty-one Years
—(Dec 5, 2012)

My feet walked another mile.
Thirty-one long winters
And my I still did not belong.
Sometimes I stumbled upon
Stones, and nigger or fucking immigrant
Cut the air like a flight of low
Flying winter birds. Time connived with
History to bind me to the eagle's back.

I would rumba, salsa, konpa, reggae, jazz & zouk
Through ports, remaining a shape shifter.
My strident steps hid the pain from knowing
My soles could not be fully rooted here.
A son who lost his compass & became acrid,
Because his mother wanted to acid
My existence into shreds of nothingness.

But my feet walked another mile.
Despite stumbling embraces here
And there, I never fully belonged.
So I danced around dreams of flight.
Fearing the lashes of dominating red birds,
I enveloped pages of literati in my cocoon.
I hardened, I shape-shifted, I suited,

I enunciated & still I felt the uprooting pain.

Thomas Jefferson hated Toussaint's boots.
My ancestors took steps in 1804, flinging
Sugar barons over bleeding Carib reefs,
African ribs ripped to plant white gold
Over ossified plantations. Thousands of feet
Hardened by colonial demands for coffee,
Pounding. Our tarsus rooted in the soil
Of our blood. My steps are a geographical
Blueprint of a crisscrossed world, merchants
Vend souls and bent-back field hands breed
Hybridity within the archipelago of Atlantic
Wombs. Wounded, stripped & fatherless
We are cocooned in our own black & red flag
With an erected palm tree, canons & sables.
My spine is a palm & my steps are history.
At a moment of despair, when my feet
Wanted to burn the winter roads behind,
I danced around dreams of flight,
Then a dove entered in my abode and coaxed me
From my cocoon. We floated above the cursed
Ground, only anchored to the currents
That gently reposed our wearied feet.
Thirty-one long gnawing winters treaded
& the abrasive terrain still rejects my roots.

Yet, I am an Atlantic diasporic molded & shaped

By circumstances, constantly shift-shifting
To survive parasitic waves. I may be bruised,
Or even battered by broken branches, but
My tarsus is rooted in the soil. My palm-spine
Is history. I can only take bold steps into destiny.
Now that my cells have split once more to bring
A new joy into my longing steps, I bloom again.
Another son emerges bearing a historical moniker.
His radiant eyes beam angels. I'm home.

Invocation

If you could sit underneath a cotton-silk wood
and grill a snapper to the bones, you would.

If you could summon God to help you swat flies
from the parched, begging mouths, you would.

If you could chase dandelions with a brush
and paint the reposing sun, you would.

If you could smooth out dreams of refugees
against the tides of slicking tycoons, you would.

But, the imagination flaps and falls.
Leaving incessant waves slapping rocks.

An uplifting voice breaks out: "Yes, you can do it."
You close your eyes and glide.

Only, the blue skies turned into burnt lilies,
the mockingbirds become deafening sirens.

You string your prayers, like kites, and fly them
to the stratosphere, vacant. Shock, you remove your shoes,

and descend into the waiting room of believers
enduring a cacophony of wishes and dictates.

Then you spot a French dictator, scissor-like hands
you avoid shaking. Your eyes scan the room of flesh-traders

flipping verses, you try to remember history as you watch
flippant redeemers pastorate with the Conquistadors' swords.

You close your eyes trying to switch channels, frantic.
But the flame of the burning monk forces you to pray.

The Magic of Rhythm
For YK, RP, ME,

I will study you,
Angiograph your arteries
Of imagination like talking drums.
Drum-talking my syllables to
The apex of cortices, until ears bleed
Their stubbornness to foreign rhythms—
Since there are no calabash trees in Amherst,
And you—never saw a moor—
Not even the sea, then you will misread
My temperamental waves that gush
Agonies like moaning whales.

You, rhythmic master, you make sparrows
Dance on naked branches. You, canvas
Painter, heighten the blues of blue jays
And the reds of cardinals. In the pale
Light of gloomy nights, you induce clarity.
I will study by rote the murmur of your breathing
As I unpack the cadence of a tailored sorcerer.
In this land of Bishop, Dickinson, and Frost
I will not be a scarecrow in a shawl.

I was not baptized by a bishop,
And no deacons ushered in my pulse.

Cantor of the Irish Spring
In memory of Seamus Heaney 1939-2013

With keen, incisive sight, you witnessed limbs
Torn from their roots as elements countered
The Crown, and the pecking orders of crows.
You crossed yourself, knowing the long, searing
Sufferings of the Celts—robbed, split over crossed-bars,
Boundary lines, imported crucifixes; however small—
Soldiering a splintered identity,
A way of cupping, cuffing the land.

Your mind 'was its own bull-pen'.
Your tongue ploughed the land,
Tilting and harvesting unified syllables,
A state, a mind, a state of mind, a multi-vocal
Irishness that silences spiteful nozzles, muddles through
Your incessant drinking from the brain's rain, a reign.

You entered a chorus of departed poets,
Their tongues permanently lit for recitals
To the gods. Lucid images and lingering sounds
Planted permanent pews inside us. Language remains
A host for our inexhaustible communion. We praised
Your rhythm of rain through a canopy of poignant syllables.

No starched flag, nor barbwire
governed your tongue. You wintered out
the old snows that cracked fertile land,
And with your plough-like pen, you dug for verdant
Earth as you squared your lines into ameliorative spaces
Of the field of force. Commodious poet,
Herculean earthman who libated with raindrops,
And comforted Ireland with your tending plough.

Poetry was your religion; you became
A liniment of a poet— constant and astute.
You became a touchable and luminous garden spirit.
You entered history unswaying, unwavering
Leaving us a language of fresh mint.

Boston Capitol Steps, 1987

In memory of Antoine Thurel

Somewhere in this ancient town, you stepped
From a bath smelling of coconuts and limes.
Your 56-year-old body—the age my father was
In the Fall of 1986—earthly black and smooth,
Concealing the pain from numerous Boston winters.
Over the years, you smugly stepped onto Beacon.

Preoccupied with work and an eventual return
To your troubled land, you were troubled by the states
And its beacon—an eagle that refuses to share
Earth's bounties. You decided to be the sun
On the footsteps of the Capitol where Charles
Sumner's 1871 Haitian Medal of Freedom hung.

You too longed for freedom, a season unbroken,
azaleas and hibiscus swaying in honeyed wind,
children with paper-thin kites streaking the sky,
untethered by the hungers of Southern planters,
and unshadowed by hog farmers' sea of fields.
History loomed, cigar-smoke curling under colonnades,
tanks grinding fruit stalls into pulp, charred pearls.

When your knees kissed concrete just before
seven, your fingers reached not for the rosary beads
but for the cannister—your hands steady, resolved.
The air thickened with the scent of industry. Flames
leapt, twenty feet, as commuters begged for mercy.
Your seared body inscribed its last manifesto—Dear
Sam—upon the fragmented and tainted granite steps.

Over the Salt & Pepper Bridge

A softness to Boston's skyline,
despite the clanking, the grinding of iron
wheels as the Red Line crosses the Salt
& Pepper Bridge—my black-bodied camera
rests in my left palm. My right hand gripping.
Index finger on the trigger—I shoot.

Vaulting to a digital chamber, the red, yellow, the purple
hues bounce off the Prudential's blue glass windows,
off the Hancock, over onto the Charles River. They highlight
the city for the night. A man in uniform probes my presence,
as if every colored person or foreign tongue wanted
some repeat of 9/11. I point to the departing sun,

The dark veil settling over the sky, the lights,
still dim. A landscape for all, patrolled by some.
My camera is a threat. I hold back the River
from flowing through my eyes. I point to the Asian
tourists, fluttering like butterflies, fawning over images
they'll share with their friends. I shoot the edge.
I shoot the lights.

Supreme

I will séance America into a love
even the Supremes will be afraid of. Court me,
angle and anchor me to rights, not to the right.

The right is afraid of supreme rights.
Dreams have fangs. Have teeth.
The court silences the hissing of riders,

and marchers for rights, gagging
the actions of the X-King,
hexing color to a supreme nothing.

Stop in the name of love we are supremely
hurt in the land of supremacy with hooded rage
snuffing rights. Hoods simmering into gloom.

America, let me séance you into a love
supreme so right that rights are
sealed by the supreme of courts.

Let me court you into a real
American love, a supreme riff
of baby love, 'til injustice do us part.

Illumination, A Sonnet

In every room, lit candles softly blaze,
Vanilla scents the air, a fragrant thread,
While in the bath, you bask in glowing rays,
Illuminating all with warmth widespread.

My legs, with sudden urge, begin to roam,
Though chill outside, I wear just simple clothes,
A t-shirt, pajama pants, within our home,
On hardwood floors, I pace where history flows.

Two generations past, we'd be denied,
From these Italian, Portuguese domains,
But now this flat, with art and hues inside,
Supports our love, transcending ancient pains.

You smiled, a candle held in tender hand,
Together, warm, in love's bright light, we stand.

Terra Blanca

Zealous men parading under
white sheets, twisting their tongues
to spit words from the shallow graves
of their bourbon-stained mouths.

I live in a country of zombies,
they don't know they are zombies.
Millions of them inhabit this land,
imbalanced by the scale of black bodies
weighed on trees, and burnt churches
and towns inscribed on their chests.

Raucous and provincial, they testify
their love for bullets. As zombies, trying
to replicate the human voice, they grunt,
but their vocal chords have been singed
by the word "NIG…NIG…NIGGER".

Too much burnt flesh,
shot flesh, hung flesh.
Zombies on galloping stallions
crossing white picket fences
to go lay on fluffed cotton bedding
with the smell of charred magnolia.

Hate is the crown of their ambitions,
a motivating desire to sweep the ashen
past from plantation beating bones.

Scorching Dreams

You were once an Atlantic beacon
that lit dreams for enchained bodies—singing
your name with hopeful notes: Haiti, Hayiti, Ayiti.

Now, voices are choked with lumps of burning
coal in black throats. Someone is scorching you
alive, mirroring the way plantations were charred.

Someone is sipping Scotch, smooth, dark ember,
blended malt, sharp on the throat. There's
money to be made on your back. Your gut is filled

with minerals, while your children gag
on Scotch Bonnet. Someone is drinking Scotch,
hooding the future with boys like wolves.

In broad daylight, hopeless men, turning werewolves
hunt their own shadows in depleted streets
where babies cast glances towards elsewhere.

You, Haiti, were once a beacon, a haven
for all backs carved by whips of unfreedom. Now,
your hand-wringing children flee with hearts ablaze.

Home, a Desire

I feel like a kite needing
its string unraveled.
Where would I fly to?

Darkness blankets the sky
before night falls,
outside turns bitter cold.

Homebound, would I take a route
in the sky into warm air of childhood,
crushed shells mixed with fine sand—

meters of desert by the sea. Hot under foot,
the smell of lemon-seasoned red snapper,
and boiled crabs in a well-spiced gumbo stew.

I'm reminded to be patient. The time
will come when home becomes an intimate
abode under welcoming and safe skies.

Patience is a poem, a need for Prometheus
to place fire on the tongue, offering songs
to enchanting ears, lobbing an opening.

Patience is a serene walk alone.
Neither terse nor hurried steps,
measured meters like a slow tug.

Perhaps I must halt my desire
to fly like a kite, or a voyager
pigeon without destination.

Darkness envelops this town

where I live. It is not home.
I've been mordantly told to go home,

like a relentless song,
like an overplayed album—
scratched with irreparable grooves.

Author photo by Menelik Sylvain

Patrick Sylvain is a Haitian-American educator, poet, writer, social and literary critic, and translator whose work explores Haiti and the Haitian diaspora's culture, politics, language, and religion. The author of several poetry collections in English and Haitian, Sylvain's poems have been nominated for the Pushcart Prize and appear in leading journals including *Ploughshares, Callaloo, Transition, Prairie Schooner, Agni, American Poetry Review, The Caribbean Writer,* and *African American Review*. He holds degrees from UMass-Boston, Harvard, Boston University, and Brandeis University, where he was the Shirle Dorothy Robbins Creative Writing Prize Fellow. Sylvain teaches Global, Transnational, and Postcolonial Literature at Simmons University and recently served on Harvard's History and Literature Tutorial Board. His publications include *Education Across Borders* (Beacon Press, 2022) and *Underworlds* (Central Square Press, 2018). Forthcoming works include *Scorched Pearl of the Antilles* (Palgrave Macmillan, 2026) and poetry collections from Central Square, and Finishing Line presses (2026).

Books by

ARROWSMITH PRESS

Girls by Oksana Zabuzhko

Bula Matari/Smasher of Rocks by Tom Sleigh

This Carrying Life by Maureen McLane

Cries of Animals Dying by Lawrence Ferlinghetti

Animals in Wartime by Matiop Wal

Divided Mind by George Scialabba

The Jinn by Amira El-Zein

Bergstein
edited by Askold Melnyczuk

Arrow Breaking Apart by Jason Shinder

Beyond Alchemy by Daniel Berrigan

Conscience, Consequence: Reflections on Father Daniel Berrigan
edited by Askold Melnyczuk

Ric's Progress by Donald Hall

Return To The Sea by Etnairis Rivera

The Kingdom of His Will by Catherine Parnell

Eight Notes from the Blue Angel by Marjana Savka

Fifty-Two by Melissa Green

Music In—And On—The Air by Lloyd Schwartz

Magpiety by Melissa Green

Reality Hunger by William Pierce

Soundings: On The Poetry of Melissa Green
edited by Sumita Chakraborty

The Corny Toys by Thomas Sayers Ellis

Black Ops by Martin Edmunds

Museum of Silence by Romeo Oriogun

City of Water by Mitch Manning

Passeggiate by Judith Baumel

Persephone Blues by Oksana Lutsyshyna

The Uncollected Delmore Schwartz
edited by Ben Mazer

The Light Outside by George Kovach

The Blood of San Gennaro by Scott Harney
edited by Megan Marshall

No Sign by Peter Balakian

Firebird by Kythe Heller

The Selected Poems of Oksana Zabuzhko
edited by Askold Melnyczuk

The Age of Waiting by Douglas J. Penick

Manimal Woe by Fanny Howe

Crank Shaped Notes by Thomas Sayers Ellis

The Land of Mild Light by Rafael Cadenas
edited by Nidia Hernández

The Silence of Your Name: The Afterlife of a Suicide by Alexandra Marshall

Flame in a Stable by Martin Edmunds

Mrs. Schmetterling by Robin Davidson

This Costly Season by John Okrent

Thorny by Judith Baumel

The Invisible Borders of Time: Five Female Latin American Poets
edited by Nidia Hernández

Some of You Will Know by David Rivard

The Forbidden Door: The Selected Poetry of Lasse Söderberg
tr. by Lars Gustaf Andersson & Carolyn Forché

Unrevolutionary Times by Houman Harouni

Between Fury & Peace: The Many Arts of Derek Walcott
edited by Askold Melnyczuk

The Burning World by Sherod Santos

Today is a Different War: Poetry of Lyudmyla Khersonska
tr. by Olga Livshin, Andrew Janco, Maya Chhabra, & Lev Fridman

Salvage by Richard Kearney

In the Hour of War: Poetry From Ukraine
edited by Carolyn Forché and Ilya Kaminsky

A Crash Course in Molotov Cocktails: Poetry of Halyna Kruk
tr. by Amelia Glaser and Yuliya Ilchuk

Don't Close Your Eyes by Hanna Melnyczuk

Tiny Extravaganzas by Diane Mehta

Departures from Rilke by Steven Cramer

On the Road to Lviv by Christopher Merrill
tr. into Ukrainian by Nina Murray

Nothing Bad Has Ever Happened
A Bouquet to Victoria Amelina

The Farewell Light by Nidia Hernández

Downfall of the Straight Line by Charles O. Hartman

The God of Freedom by Yulia Musakovska
tr. Olena Jennings and the author

Away Away by Mark Pawlak

The Miró Worm and the Mysteries of Writing by Sven Birkerts

St. Matthew Passion by Gjertrud Schnackenberg

New and Selected Poems by Glyn Maxwell

A Precise Chaos by Jo-Ann Mort

Where Do You Live? by Jennifer Jean

Coming Ashore by Thomas O'Grady

Crimean Fig / Qırım İnciri
edited by Anastasia Levkova, Askold Melnyczuk,
& Nataliya Shpylova-Saeed

Hungry Ghost by Bruce Smith

At the Same Time by Wang Jiaxin
tr. by John Balcom

The Scent of Man by Tadeusz Dąbrowski
tr. by Antonia Lloyd-Jones

World on a String by Gail Mazur

Artur Schnabel and Joseph Szigeti Play Mozart at the Frick Collection (April 14, 1948) and other poems by Lloyd Schwartz

ARROWSMITH is named after the late William Arrowsmith, a renowned classics scholar, literary and film critic. General editor of thirty-three volumes of *The Greek Tragedy in New Translations*, he was also a brilliant translator of Eugenio Montale, Cesare Pavese, and others. Arrowsmith, who taught for years in Boston University's University Professors Program, championed not only the classics and the finest in contemporary literature, he was also passionate about the importance of recognizing the translator's role in bringing the original work to life in a new language.

Like the arrowsmith who turns his arrows straight and true, a wise person makes his character straight and true.

— Buddha

www.ingramcontent.com/pod-product-compliance
Lightning Source LLC
LaVergne TN
LVHW041608070526
838199LV00052B/3045